WHERE DID MY ROOMMATE PUT MY CHARGER?

A KIND-OF ACTIVITY BOOK FOR KIND-OF ADULTS.

SARAH KEMPA

Andrews McMeel
PUBLISHING®

Andrews McMeel Publishing
a division of Andrews McMeel Universal
1130 Walnut Street, Kansas City, Missouri 64106

www.andrewsmcmeel.com

22 23 24 25 26 RLP 10 9 8 7 6 5 4 3 2 1

ISBN: 978-1-5248-6901-4

Editor: Allison Adler
Art Director: Holly Swayne
Production Editor: Julie Railsback
Production Manager: Tamara Haus

ATTENTION: SCHOOLS AND BUSINESSES
Andrews McMeel books are available at quantity discounts with bulk purchase
for educational, business, or sales promotional use. For information,
please e-mail the Andrews McMeel Publishing Special Sales Department:
specialsales@amuniversal.com.

THANK YOU TO MY LOVING PARENTS, MY AGENT PAUL LUCAS, MY EDITOR ALLISON ADLER, MY DEAR FRIENDS AND CONSTANT SUPPORTERS, AND MY CONSTANT COMPANIONS/SOMETIMES EDITORS EMILY KEMPA AND JAMIE SERLIN.

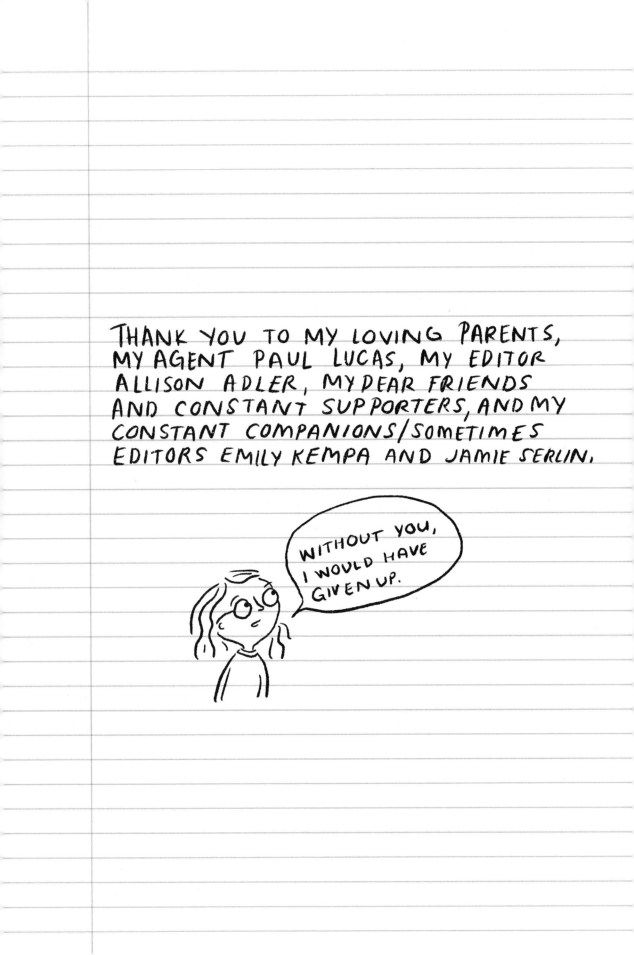

WITHOUT YOU, I WOULD HAVE GIVEN UP.

MAYBE YOU CAN USE THIS SECTION FOR HAND OCCUPANCY?

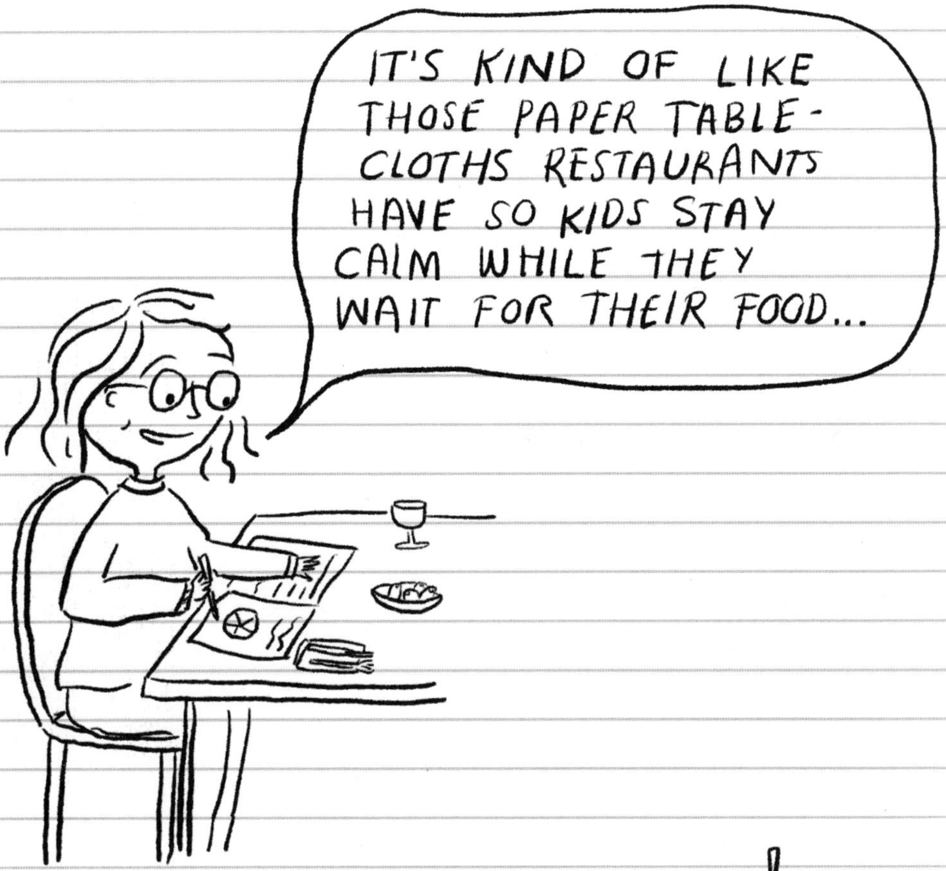

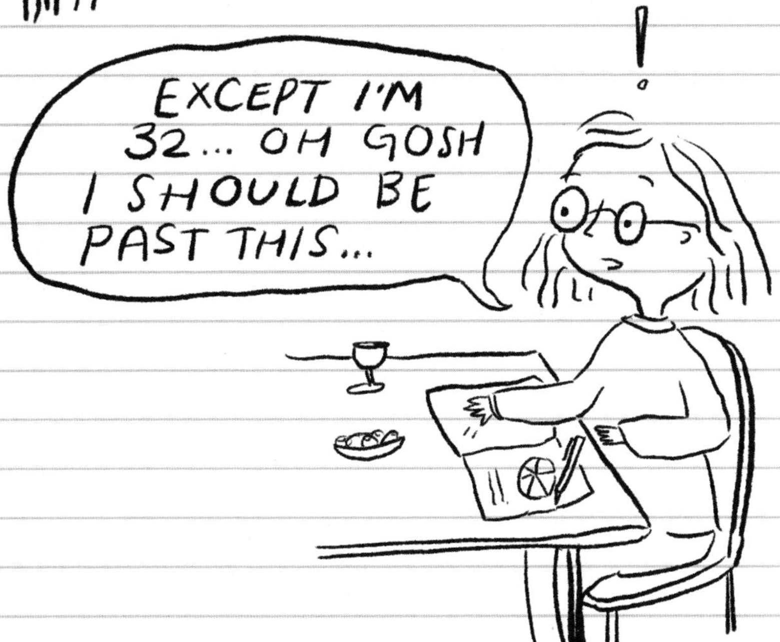

HIP AND TRENDY RESTAURANT
CAN YOU FIND?

- SOMEONE NURSING A DRINK AND A CRUSH ON THE BARTENDER.
- SOMEONE JUST NOTICING THEIR EX HAS MOVED ON.
- SOMEONE TRYING TO SPLIT THE CHECK.
- PARENTS IN TOWN VISITING THEIR DAUGHTER, PRETENDING TO LOVE DUCK CONFIT.
- A PROLIFIC MANSPLAINER.
- A VACATION SLIDESHOW.

TOILET

5

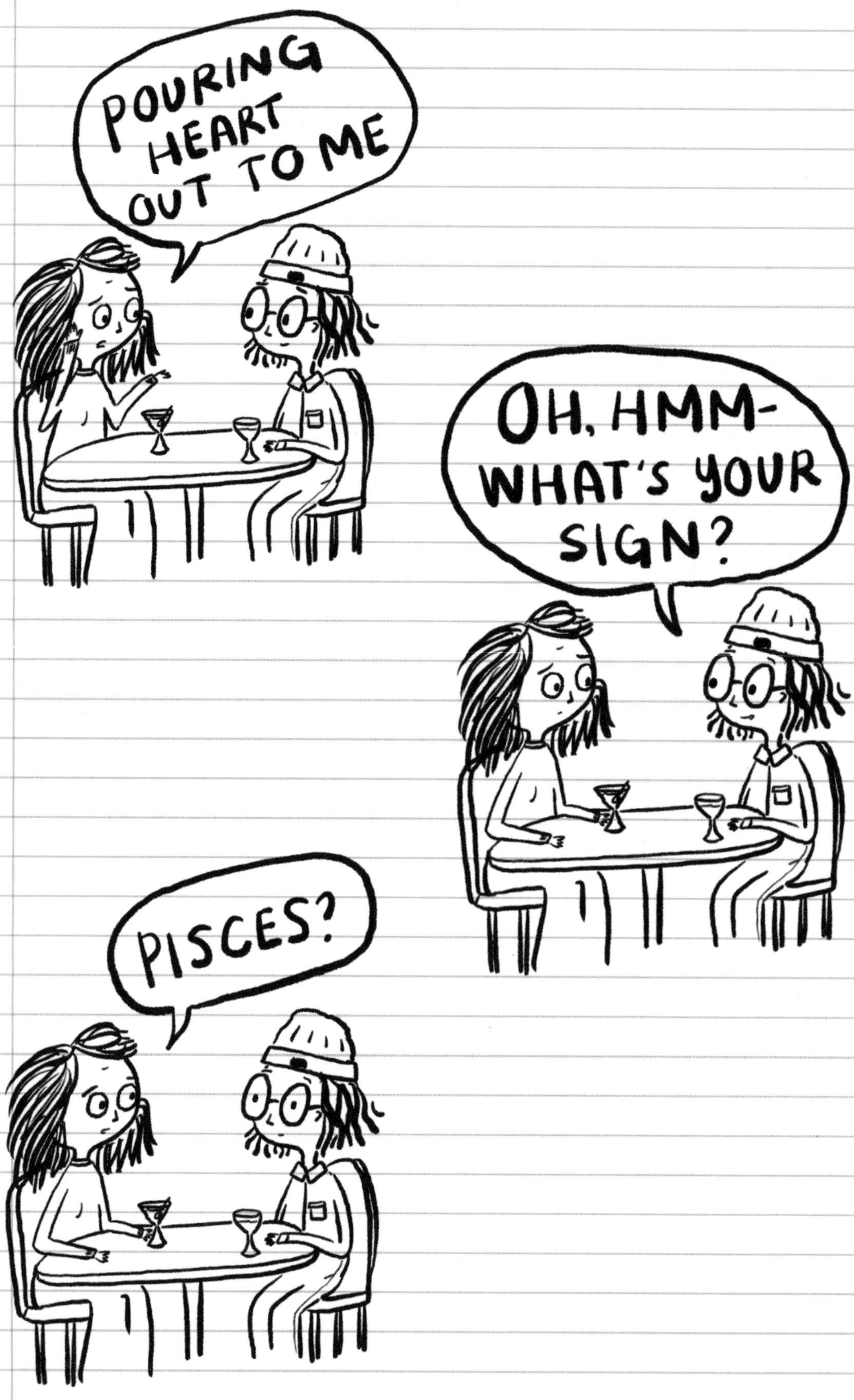
POURING HEART OUT TO ME
OH, HMM- WHAT'S YOUR SIGN?
PISCES?

WHEN DOES EACH ZODIAC SIGN
SHOW UP TO MEET SOMEONE?
FILL IN THE BLANKS TO FIND OUT!

NOW!

EXACTLY ON TIME, NOT A MINUTE BEFORE OR A MINUTE AFTER.

☺ MAYBE SHOWS, MAYBE DOESN'T. ☹

40 MINUTES LATE BUT BROUGHT THE PARTY.

AN HOUR LATE BUT PAYS FOR DRINKS.

TODAY
8-9 PM
DRINKS WITH LUCY!

ON TIME, IT'S ON THEIR SCHEDULE!

BE THERE IN 15 MIN!!!!
SORRYYY!!!

15 MINUTES LATE BUT ALWAYS TEXTS FIRST!

HELLO

ARE YOU IMPORTANT?

10 MINUTES EARLY IF YOU ARE IMPORTANT, LATE IF THEY HAVE SOMETHING MORE IMPORTANT TO DO.

WHAT IS TIME?

CAN WE MAKE ROOM FOR ONE MORE?

15 MINUTES LATE AND WITH ANOTHER PERSON.

YOU ALL LOOK AMAZING!!

30 MINUTES LATE BUT BEAMING WITH CONTAGIOUS POSITIVITY.

AN HOUR LATE BUT LOOKS STUNNING.

Hi! I'M HERE!

LATE AND ALSO CRYING.

SPLIT THIS CHECK!

> SHOULD WE SPLIT THIS EQUALLY?

> VENMO ME?

> YOUR ORDER!

> WHAT'S THE TOTAL?

> HOW MUCH FOR ME?

RESTAURANT THAT MOSTLY SERVES SMALL PLATES

BAR AND GRILL

TABLE # 3
TRANSACTION #: 69136
SERVER: LAUREN
Cust: SEVERAL

3	MEZCAL	$39
2	MAI TAI	$26
4	SPRITZ	$52
1	NEGRONI	$16
1	CRISPY POTATOES	$9
2	HERB FRIES	$18
1	BRUSSELS	$11
1	CAULIFLOWER	$11
2	OYSTERS	$36
1	TARTINE BREAD	$14
3	SMOKED TROUT	$60
1	CHICKEN	$23
1	SHORT RIB	$29
1	CHOCOLATE TART	$11

TOTAL : $355
TIP : $71
INCLUDED

GRAND TOTAL: $426.00

CAN YOU SPLIT THIS CHECK FOR EACH OF THE FOLLOWING SCENARIOS?

- AMONG A GROUP OF FRIENDS FOR A BIRTHDAY DINNER (REMEMBER BIRTHDAY PERSON DOESN'T PAY!): _____

- ON A FIRST DATE: _____

- ON LIKE THE THOUSANDTH DATE WITH THE SAME PERSON: _____

- WITH SOMEONE WHO ASKED TO "PICK YOUR BRAIN": _____

- WITH YOUR FRIEND WHO HAS BEEN SLEEPING ON YOUR COUCH FOR GOING ON TWO MONTHS: _____

- AMONG A GROUP OF FRIENDS WHO ORDERED SOME THINGS FOR THE TABLE EVEN IF YOU DIDN'T EAT ANY OF IT.
  - IF YOU STILL WANT TO BE FRIENDS: _____
  - IF YOU DECIDE YOU DON'T REALLY LIKE THESE FRIENDS ANYMORE: _____

COSMICALLY IDEAL PIZZA TOPPINGS

FILL IN THE BLANKS TO FIND OUT EACH ZODIAC SIGN'S PIZZA TOPPING.

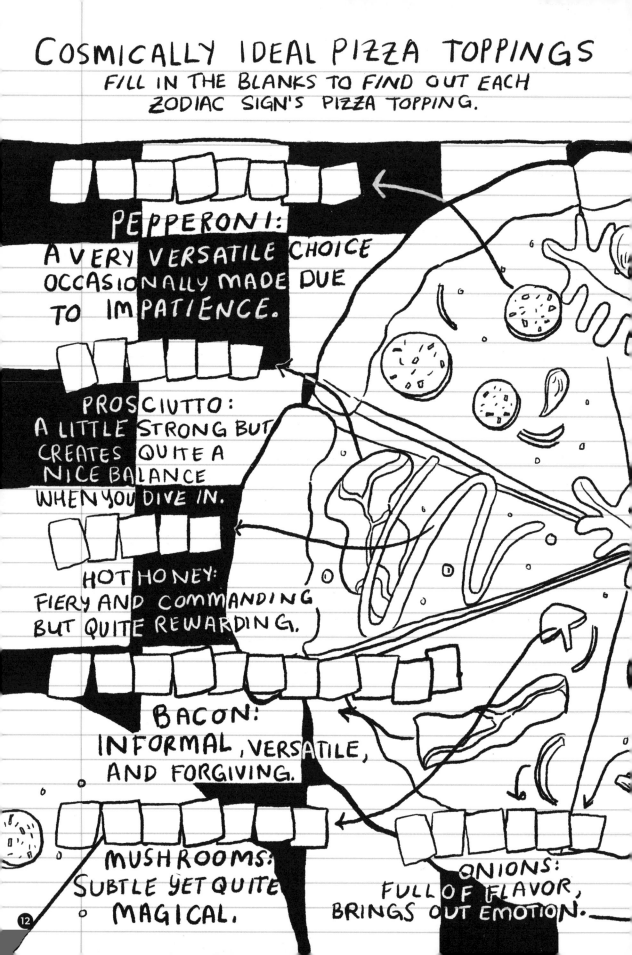

PEPPERONI:
A VERY VERSATILE CHOICE OCCASIONALLY MADE DUE TO IMPATIENCE.

PROSCIUTTO:
A LITTLE STRONG BUT CREATES QUITE A NICE BALANCE WHEN YOU DIVE IN.

HOT HONEY:
FIERY AND COMMANDING BUT QUITE REWARDING.

BACON:
INFORMAL, VERSATILE, AND FORGIVING.

MUSHROOMS:
SUBTLE YET QUITE MAGICAL.

ONIONS:
FULL OF FLAVOR, BRINGS OUT EMOTION.

PINEAPPLE: FUN AND BELOVED BY SOME, BUT HIGHLY POLARIZING.

PEPPER: MAY SEEM BLAND BUT REALLY IS MOST INTENTIONAL.

ARUGULA: LIKABLE AND SIMPLE, YET SOMEHOW NEVER CEASES TO IMPRESS.

GARLIC: DEMANDING BUT RADIANT AND REGAL.

FRESH PEAS: SURE, MAYBE COMES ACROSS AS A LITTLE STRANGE BUT REALLY QUITE IMAGINATIVE.

TOMATOES: SUBTLE AND PRAGMATIC, THE FOUNDATION OF PIES.

JUST SOME
WINE ETIQUETTE TIPS

WHILE ON A DATE...

THE 4 S'S:

SWIRL, SNIFF, SWISH, SWISH!

WOW! SO... CRISP/FLORAL/ROCKY/EARTHY/FULL! (PICK ONE.)

WHILE WITH FRIENDS...

YOUR CHEAPEST BOTTLE PLEASE.

WHILE AT HOME...

IN A MASON JAR ALONGSIDE AN EPISODE OF LOVE ISLAND.

I GOT A TEXT!!

WHILE AT A CHURCH...

ONE SIP, ONE NOD.

OH, WINE? AAAAMEN.

AT A WEDDING... BOTTOMLESS.

AH, YES - THE BRIDE IS SO BEAUTIFUL... THIS CHARDONNAY? GOOD ENOUGH. I'LL HAVE ANOTHER.

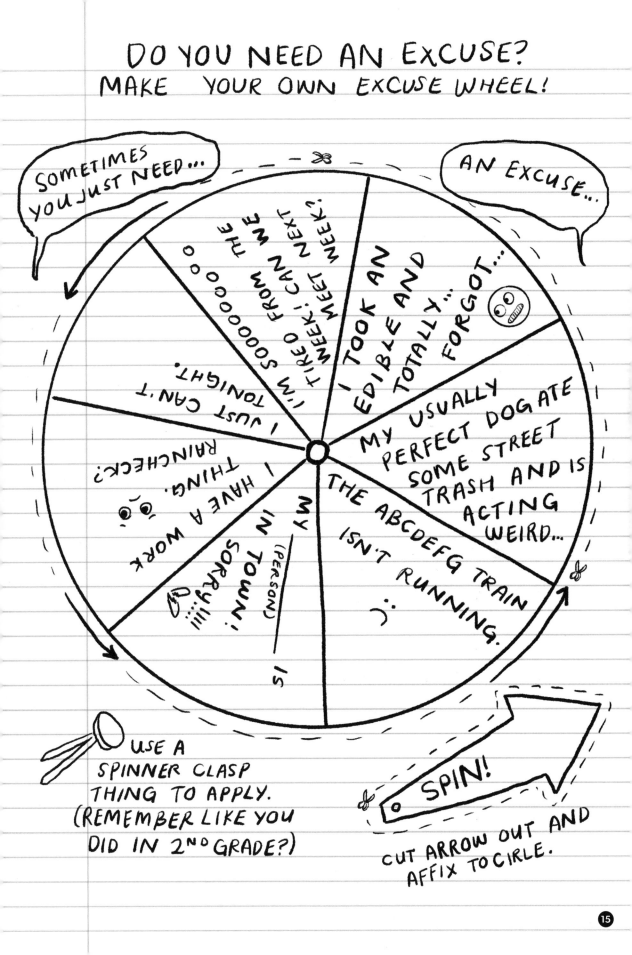

THIS PAGE INTENTIONALLY LEFT BLANK.

YOU KNOW... FOR THE EXCUSE WHEEL...

TWO HOURS LATER...

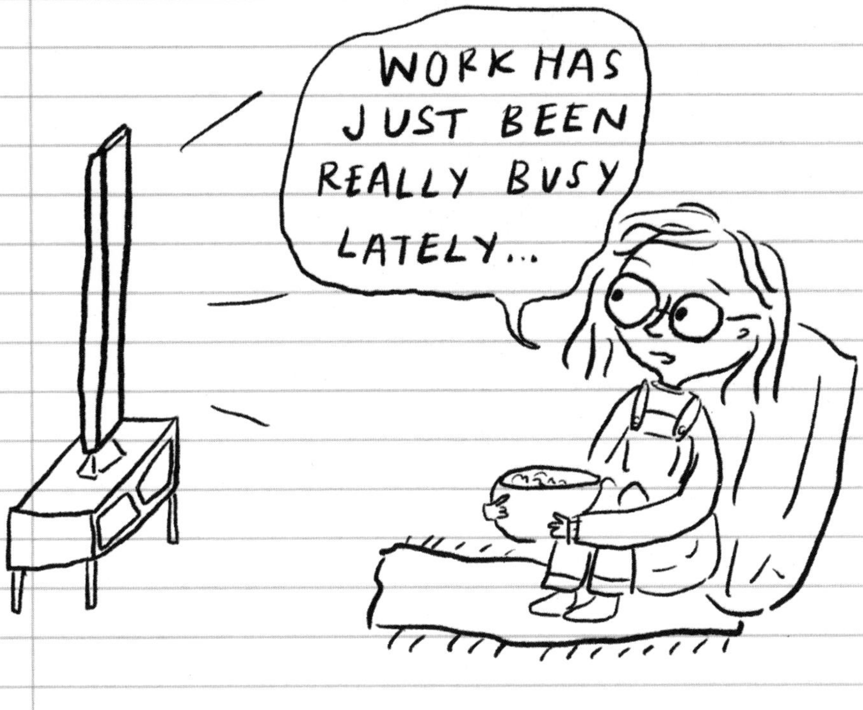

DATING APPS

CAN YOU FIND?

- SOMEONE NOT NAMED SEAN, JARED, BRIAN, OR CHAD.

- SOMEONE WHO IS DEFINITELY 6 FEET TALL.

- A PHOTO THAT MAY BE BEST LEFT UNOPENED.

- AN UNINSPIRING QUOTE FROM "THE OFFICE."

- WHICH OF THE 8 PEOPLE IN THIS PHOTO IS JESSICA.

ROBERT

AMANDA

BELIEVE IT OR NOT THIS IS A PHOTO OF ME WITH YOUR EX! ALSO MY EX!

"WOULD I RATHER BE FEARED OR LOVED? EASY. BOTH. I WANT PEOPLE TO BE AFRAID OF HOW MUCH THEY LOVE ME."

🧁 33 6'0" 📍NYC

💼 BUSINESS GUY

MATCHES

JARED B.
!! Hey cutie!!

JARED C.
Hey!! How are you?-

CHAD A.
How's your night?

SEAN C.
Hey

BRIAN D.
What's up?

JARED F.

JESSICA, 29

Messages

SEARCH

Sam   20min Ago
hello cutie

Daniel   1 hr ago
Come over for
a glass of wine.

Charlie
Sent a photo.
;)

Zak

YOU'VE RUN OUT
OF MATCHES!
MAYBE EXPAND YOUR
DISTANCE OR ...
LOWER YOUR STANDARDS.
..

CREATE THE PERFECT PROFILE FOR YOUR DATING APP

BE SURE TO INCLUDE...

- A DOG!
- A TIGER!
- A FISH!

I'M TIRED OF BEING USED...

- A BEACH WITH CRYSTAL CLEAR WATER!
- ALSO A CLIFF THOUGH!
- MAYBE THE VIEW FROM A MOUNTAIN?
- A SWIMSUIT!
- BUT ALSO SKIS AND SNOWSUIT!
- A TODDLER! (BUT NOT YOUR OWN!)
- AN "OFFICE" QUOTE!
- WHILE MAKING IT ALL RELATABLE AND DOWN TO EARTH.

YOUR NAME   AGE

ABOUT YOU:

GRAB A PEN AND DRAW HERE.

WOW! A SWIPE RIGHT FOR ME!

SWIPE
SWIPE
BAGUETTE
1 DAY OLD
OOOOOOOO!
WELL, WELL
WHAT DO WE
HAVE HERE...?

POOF!
BUZZ BUZZ
7:00 pm
WORK
Hey! Did you have a chance to update the deck for tomorrow??
TIME TO GET THAT BREAD...

SPOT THE DIFFERENCE IN JARED'S DATING PROFILES

PEOPLE ARE ALWAYS LIKE
"DON'T WAIT FOR SOMEONE ELSE,
DATE YOURSELF!"

ALL LIKE:
"TREAT YOURSELF TO DINNER AND DRINKS,
BUY YOURSELF A GIFT, BLAH BLAH BLAH..."

AND IT'S LIKE...

I'M PROBABLY SPENDING TOO MUCH ON CANDLES ACTUALLY...
I NEED TO STOP BUYING GIFTS FOR MYSELF...
!!
I NEED TO BREAK UP WITH MYSELF.

APARTMENT
CAN YOU FIND?

- SPARE TOILET PAPER ARTFULLY STOWED.
- A DEAD COCKROACH WAITING TO BE FOUND.
- 7 WATER GLASSES THAT HAVE BEEN ACCUMULATING OVER THE WEEK.
- A MISSING PUZZLE PIECE.
- PHONE, KEYS, WALLET!
- YOUR CHARGER!!

DO YOU EVER FIND YOURSELF
STARING OFF INTO THE
DISTANCE, DAYDREAMING...

... INTO THE BACK OF YOUR FRIDGE?

LIKE AMONGST THE
COOL AIR IT HOLDS
ALL OF YOUR DREAMS?

I MEAN... IT DOES. IT HOLDS MY WINE, MY CHEESE, MY SELTZERS, MY...
MILK

THANK YOU, FRIDGE.

I JUST CAN'T HAVE YOU LIVING HERE AND NOT PAYING RENT...
MAYBE YOU COULD CHIP IN ON SOME CHORES? DISHES, CLEANING, GARBAGE?
HAVE YOU EVER SEEN A ROACH FLY?
(FAINTS)

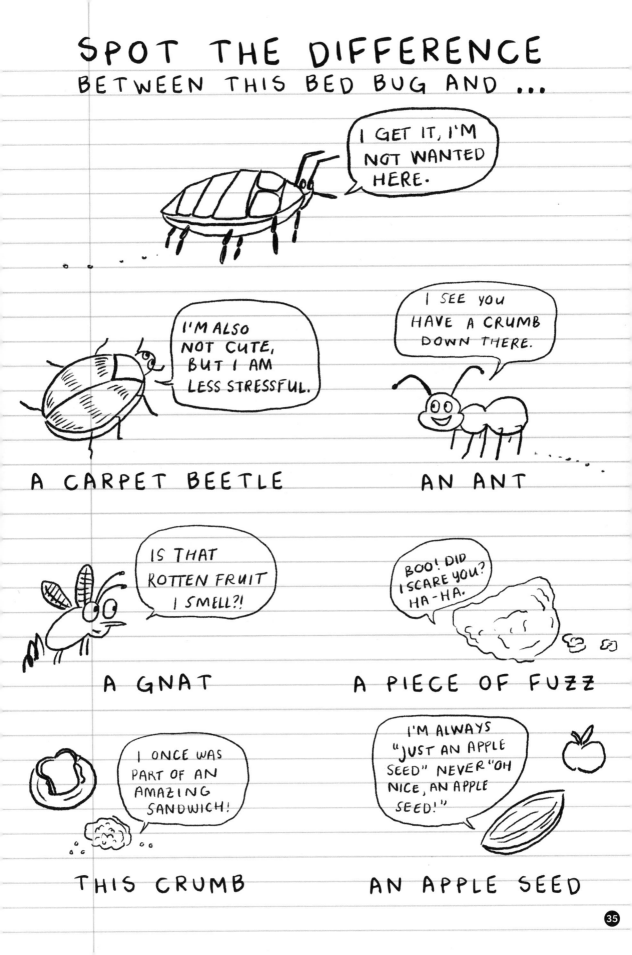

ONCE I HAD A PANIC ATTACK WHILE MY ROOMMATE WAS OUT OF TOWN.

WHEN SHE RETURNED, WE WERE DISCUSSING:

DO YOU KNOW WHAT CAUSED IT?

NO, NOT REALLY.

NO, I DON'T THINK SO...

WAS IT WORK RELATED?

TIME MANAGEMENT?

I HONESTLY THINK IT WAS BECAUSE I WAS THINKING ABOUT HOW FOR ALMOST ALL OF ETERNITY I DID NOT EXIST AND MY CELLS ARE ALIVE FOR SUCH A SMALL SLIVER OF TIME BEFORE I GO BACK TO NOT EXISTING.
AND I REALIZED I WILL NEVER KNOW WHAT IT FEELS LIKE, YOU KNOW?
CASHEW?

CONFIGURE THIS STUDIO APARTMENT FLOOR PLAN INTO A TWO BEDROOM APARTMENT

EVER FIND YOURSELF LIVING IN A BEDROOM THAT HAD NO WINDOWS? OR WALLS THAT STOPPED A FEW FEET BELOW THE CEILING? LIKELY THE WORK OF A CREATIVE REAL ESTATE BROKER...
CREATE YOUR OWN PERFECT LITTLE TWO BEDROOM CONVERTED APARTMENT BY ADDING SOME TEMPORARY WALLS THAT ARE DEFINITELY NOT ILLEGAL FIRE HAZARDS AND MOVE ON IN.

CAN YOU CONFRONT YOUR ROOMMATE ABOUT EVERYTHING THAT'S BEEN BUILDING UP AND CAUSING TENSION BETWEEN YOU TWO?

COMPLETE THE SENTENCES.

MEDIUM: IN PERSON   TEXT   EMAIL
(PICK ONE)

DO YOU HAVE A FEW MINUTES?_____I WANTED TO
                              (INSERT EMOJI)

_____ SOMETHING BY YOU
       (VERB)

THAT'S BEEN BOTHERING ME. I _____
                                    (VERB)

LIVING WITH YOU AND WANT OUR _____ TO
                                  (NOUN)

CONTINUE, BUT IT _____ ME
                          (VERB)

THAT YOU _____ .
(INSERT OFFENSES. I.E. NEVER TAKE GARBAGE OUT, LEAVE YOUR
EMPTY BOXES FOR WEEKS, NEVER EMPTY THE DISHWASHER, NEVER
CLEAN THE BATHROOM, LEAVE YOUR TAMPONS IN THE TRASH FOR
WEEKS, LEAVE ROTTING FOOD IN FRIDGE ETC...)

IT MAKES ME FEEL _____ .
                        (DESCRIPTIVE NOUN LIKE SAD,
                   DISRESPECTED, ANGRY, THIS EMOJI- 😖)

CAN YOU NOT?

_____ ,
(MESSAGE SIGN OFF,
ANYTHING BESIDES
"THANKS!" REALLY)

_____
(YOUR NAME)

COMMUNICATION IS KEY!

ZODIAC SIGNS' BIGGEST
COHABITATION FAUX PAS
COMPLETE THE BLANKS.

ALWAYS ON THE PHONE.

CONFUSED AND ANNOYED THAT THEY EVEN HAVE A ROOMMATE.

GETS ANNOYED WITH YOU OVER SOMETHING THEY DID AND JUST FORGOT ABOUT.

HAS STUFF EVERYWHERE.

QUITE CHATTY.

NEEDS TO BE INVITED EVERYWHERE BUT WON'T ACTUALLY JOIN.

INSISTS ON CHORE WHEEL.

ALWAYS HAS T.V. ON.

SIGHHHHHH! SIGHHHHHH!

LOTS OF SIGHING, CULMINATING IN ONE LARGE ARGUMENT THAT THEY PROMPTLY FORGET ABOUT.

SOMETIMES CLINGY.

I'LL JUST VENMO YOU!

HAS NO MONTHLY BILLS IN THEIR NAME.

HAS NEVER TAKEN TRASH OUT.

DO YOU EVER HAVE TROUBLE SLEEPING?
MAYBE YOU WAKE UP IN THE MIDDLE OF
THE NIGHT FEELING BOTH WIDE AWAKE
AND COMPLETELY EXHAUSTED?

YOUR HEAD
SPINNING ON
ALL THE THINGS
YOU NEED TO DO.

SOME EXPERTS RECOMMEND YOU GET UP AND DO SOMETHING LIKE STRETCHING, READING, OR KNITTING.

THAT WAY YOU CAN MULTITASK.

COFFEE SHOP

CAN YOU FIND?

- SOMEONE WATCHING SOMEONE ELSE'S STUFF.
- AN OUTLET.
- THE WIFI PASSWORD.
- AN OPEN SEAT.
- THE OAT MILK.
- THE BATHROOM KEY.

COFFEE BY ZODIAC SIGN

FILL IN THE BLANKS TO FIND OUT HOW
EACH ZODIAC SIGN GETS THEIR CAFFEINE.

ESPRESSO: CLASSIC AND
EFFICIENT.

COFFEE WITH
OAT MILK: TRENDY

INSTANT COFFEE: IMPATIENT
BUT NOT PICKY.

DECAF: DOESN'T NEED
CAFFEINE.

POUR OVER: VERY
PATIENT.

RED EYE: VERY
INTENSE.

DRIP COFFEE WITH 2 SUGARS: ROUTINE CHOICE.

NESPRESSO: FLASHY AND VERY IMPATIENT.

COLD BREW: FUN! SUMMER FOREVER!

LATTE: SOFT AND SWEET.

KEURIG: DEPENDABLE.

FRENCH PRESS: VERY STRONG.

MORNING

NOON

NIGHT

49

EXCUSE ME – CAN YOU WATCH MY THINGS?

DRAW AN ARROW TO SEE WHO'S WATCHING WHOSE THINGS TO FIGURE OUT WHOSE STUFF IS UNATTENDED.

CAN I GET YOU COFFEE AND PICK YOUR BRAIN?

COMPLETE THE SENTENCES WITH THE APPROPRIATE WORDS.

MEDIUM:
(PICK ONE)

TEXT

EMAIL

LINKEDIN

HIIIIIIIIIIIII _____ ,
(INSERT "FRIEND'S" NAME)

_____ . I SAW _____
(CORDIAL GREETING)   (THING OF INTEREST YOU SAW – A
                                 NEW JOB? A PROJECT? A PERSON?)

AND THINK IT'S SO _____ !
(ADJECTIVE)

I WAS HOPING THAT WE COULD MEET UP OVER

_____ (MY TREAT _____ !)
(CAFFEINATED BEVERAGE)   (SEVERAL EMOJIS)

AND I COULD _____ YOUR BRAIN A BIT?
(VERB)

LET ME KNOW!

_____
(SEVERAL EMOJIS)

_____
(YOUR NAME)

COFFEE?

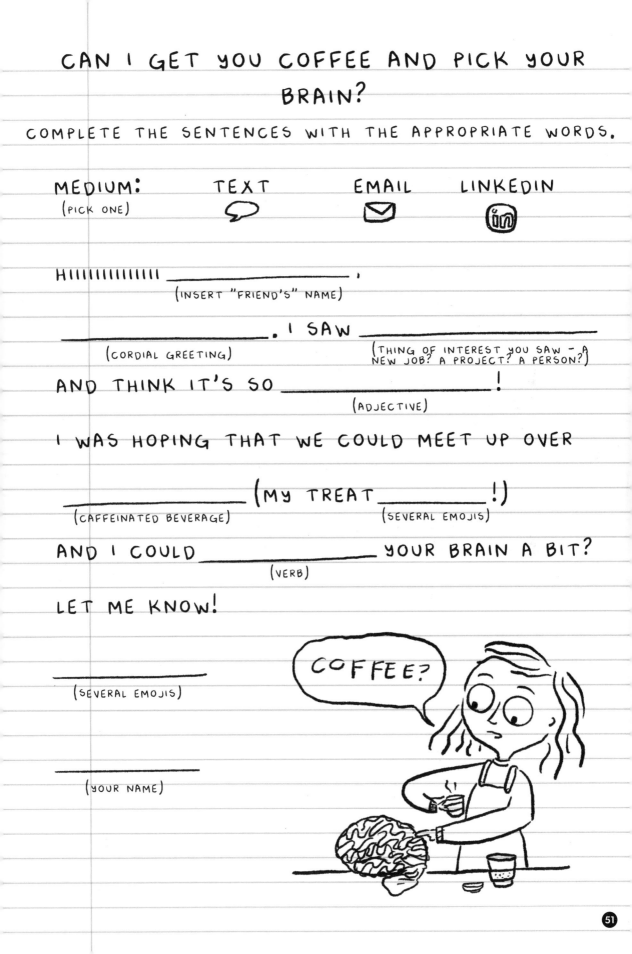

HOW TO DRAW:
AN ANXIOUS PERSON

1) START BY DRAWING A CIRCLE.

(NO NEED TO BE SYMMETRICAL!)

2) MAKE THE CIRCLE A SPHERE.

← WHERE EYES WILL GO.

3) ADD IN SHOULDERS.

4) DRAW ARMS. YOU CAN MAKE THEM CROSSED TO HOLD YOUR LEGS OR STRAIGHT TO SIT ON YOUR HANDS.

5) COMPLETE BODY.

6) CUSTOMIZE FACE AND ERASE GUIDE LINES.

7) ACCESSORIZE! ADD DETAILS LIKE MOTION LINES, CUTE SHOES, AND A CUP OF COFFEE!

AND VIOLA! CONGRATS ON THE SELF-PORTRAIT!

FARMERS' MARKET
CAN YOU FIND?

- PERSON GETTING SWARMED BY PETITIONERS.
- A COUPLE DISTRACTED DOG OWNERS.
- FOUR PEOPLE WHO COULDN'T WAIT ON THEIR FRESH BREAD.
- SOMEONE WHO FORGOT THEIR REUSABLE BAGS.
- THE ONLY PUBLIC RESTROOM.
- A BREAKUP.

FARMERS' MARKET HAULS BY ZODIAC SIGNS
WHAT'S EACH SIGN BRINGING HOME?
FILL IN THE BLANKS TO FIND OUT.

CHARMED THEIR WAY INTO GETTING A CHEESE SAMPLER AND FREE END-OF-DAY BAKED GOODS.

ARRIVED WITH A PLAN, WILL NOT BE UPSOLD! JUST GROCERIES.

GROCERIES AND TWO CHOCOLATE COOKIES, ONE FOR THEM AND ONE FOR THEIR ROOMMATE

TWO TACOS, CINNAMON ROLLS, AND AN ONION

A PIE AND BOUQUET OF FLOWERS

DROPPED OFF COMPOST AND PICKED UP TWO STINKY CHEESES AND A LOAF OF SOURDOUGH

CHEESE, BABKA, AND SEVERAL POLAROIDS OF THEIR CREW.

SHOWED UP ON WRONG DAY. :(PICKED UP A LATTE ON THEIR WAY HOME.

MAPLE SYRUP, PANCAKE MIX, AND HONEY.

ICED COFFEE, A FEW SAMPLES, AND A NEW TOTE.

A NEWSPAPER, LOAF OF SEEDY BREAD, AND FLYER FOR NEXT CB MEETING.

A SPIKY SUCCULENT, NOTHING ELSE.

REVIEWS OF KALE BASED ON ANYTHING BESIDES TASTE

COLOR ME IN!

CURLY KALE
☆☆☆
SURPRISINGLY SPRINGY, TOUGH BUT CAN LOOSEN UP WITH A QUICK MASSAGE.

LACINATO KALE
☆☆☆
DECENT FAN, GOOD BOUQUET POTENTIAL, A BIT BORING ON ITS OWN THOUGH.

REDBOR KALE
☆☆☆☆⯪
PURPLE! SEXY!

RED RUSSIAN
☆☆⯪
DIFFICULT TO KEEP INTACT.

SIBERIAN KALE
☆☆
LIKE REBOR BUT NOT PURPLE? :(

ORNAMENTAL KALE
☆☆☆☆
LIKE A SUCCULENT BUT NOT? BOLD DECORATIVE CHOICE.

PAIR CHEESES WITH ~~WINE~~ BEVERAGE

(THERE ARE NO WRONG ANSWERS.)

KRAFT SINGLES

MANCHEGO

PROVOLONE

PECORINO

ENGLISH CHEDDAR

DAIRYLEA

BLUE CHEESE

BURRATA

BRIE

LEMON SELTZER

2% MILK

GAMAY

CHARDONNAY

VODKA

PILSNER

HARD SELTZER

COFFEE

EMERGEN-C PACKET

WHAT DO YOU DO?

YOU LOCK EYES WITH A PETITIONER OUTSIDE THE PARK... THEY ARE HOLDING A CLIPBOARD AND JUST WANT A MINUTE OF YOUR TIME...

FOR THE ENVIRONMENT!

PLEEEASE!

YOU...
SMILE & NOD WALKING FASTER.
BACK AWAY SLOWLY AND LOOK FOR ANOTHER ENTRANCE.
RUN
THEY COMPLIMENT YOUR GLASSES, HAIR, OR FARMERS' MARKET CHOICE.
COOL HAIR.
GREAT GLASSES.
HEY THERE, CONFIDENT STRIDE!
YOU FORCE A SMILE
AND GIVE THEM YOUR NAME, ADDRESS, EMAIL, PHONE, SOCIAL, ETC.
YOU BREAK YOUR GLASSES AND KEEP WALKING.

HALLOWEEN DOG PARADE
CAN YOU FIND?

- DOG OWNER WHO LOST TRACK OF THEIR PUP.
- GUY TRYING TO USE HIS DOG TO GET A DATE.
- COMPETING PINEAPPLES.
- CONFIDENT JOGGER.
- A LITTLE POOP.
- LOOFAH DOG COSTUME.

New Yorker

63

FOUR HOURS EARLIER...

WHAT'S EACH DOG THINKING?

MATCH EACH THOUGHT BUBBLE TO THE CORRECT DOG.

CIRCLE THE ITEMS A DOG SHOULD NOT EAT UNDER ANY CIRCUMSTANCES!

(FROM A HUMAN'S, NOT A DOG'S, PERSPECTIVE, OBVIOUSLY!)

CHOCOLATE

STREET FOOD

GUM

AVOCADO

RAISINS

BANANA

YOUR DINNER

CARROTS

SHOELACES

BEEF

POOP

SHOES

AIRPORT TERMINAL
CAN YOU FIND?

- A MISPLACED PASSPORT.
- AN OPEN OUTLET NEAR A CHAIR OR SOME FLOOR SPACE TO CHARGE YOUR PHONE.
- UNATTENDED LUGGAGE. TSK, TSK!
- SOMEONE HEADING TO PARADISE.
- A FORGOTTEN BELT.
- A COMFORT ANIMAL? OR A PARROT?

ZODIAC SIGNS' BOARDING TENDENCIES

FILL IN THE BLANKS TO FIND OUT THE BOARDING TENDENCIES OF EACH ZODIAC SIGN.

HAS PRE-CHECK!

STANDS BY GATE AS SOON AS ANNOUNCEMENT IS MADE.

FIRST CLASS, WAITING IN THE LOUNGE.

WAITS PATIENTLY TO BOARD THEN REALIZES THEY ARE WAITING AT WRONG GATE.

ARRIVES WITH PLENTY OF TIME TO USE THE RESTROOM, FILL THEIR WATER, AND WAIT PATIENTLY WITHOUT CROWDING ANYONE.

SECOND ONLY TO FIRST CLASS, WHILE ON A CALL.

STAYS SEATED UNTIL GROUP IS CALLED, BUT THEN POWERS RIGHT TO THE FRONT OF THE LINE.

BOARDS AS GATE CLOSES.

WAITS NEAR BOARDING AREA TEN MINUTES BEFORE IT STARTS.

FIRST IS THE WORST...

SOMEHOW ALWAYS LAST BUT NOT STRESSED ABOUT IT.

GROUP 4 ON MY BOARDING PASS, GROUP 1 IN MY HEAD.

WILL BOARD WHENEVER THEY CHOOSE.

ARE WE NOW BEST FRIENDS?

STARTED A CONVERSATION WITH ANOTHER TRAVELER AND NOW IS MAYBE UPGRADED?

THERE'S EXERCISING...

WORK IT!

AND THEN THERE'S RUNNING ACROSS TWO TERMINALS WITH 15 MINUTES TO SPARE TO CATCH A FLIGHT.

WHAT'S SETTING OFF SECURITY?

CAN YOU LOCATE ALL THE ITEMS THAT ARE SETTING OFF SECURITY?

HELP THESE TRAVELERS FIND THEIR WAY TO THE RIGHT GATE.

UNTANGLE THESE CORDS

CAN YOU UNTANGLE THESE CORDS SO FOLKS CAN CATCH THEIR FLIGHTS?

GUESS WHICH ANIMALS CAN GET THEIR WINGS.

IDENTIFY WHICH ANIMALS CAN FLY IN THE CABIN AS COMFORT ANIMALS.

I TRAVEL PRETTY LIGHT - JUST MY SHELL AND SOME COMIC BOOKS.
TURTLE
CAN SOMEONE GIVE ME A HAND?
SPIDERS
HEDGEHOG
I'M PRE-CHECK.
PEACOCK
PIG

DON'T FORGET! YOU'RE AT THE AIRPORT!

A CRYING TRAVELER WHO HAS BEEN AT THE AIRPORT FOR OVER TEN HOURS AND JUST WANTS TO GET HOME.

ANOTHER CRYING TRAVELER WHO JUST MISSED THEIR FLIGHT.

YET ANOTHER TRAVELER CRYING BECAUSE THEY JUST SAW A CUTE FAMILY WALK BY AND THEY'RE NOT SURE WHEN THEY'LL SEE THEIR OWN FAMILY AGAIN.

A TRAVELER CRYING BECAUSE THEY REALIZED THEY SHOULDN'T HAVE EATEN THAT DOUBLE PATTY WITH CHEESE AND CARAMELIZED ONIONS BEFORE THEIR INTERNATIONAL FLIGHT.

CAN YOU PAIR EACH OF THESE WITH THE CORRECT NUMBER?

NO NEED TO BE A MATHEMATICIAN HERE, TRUST YOUR GUT!

CARBON EMISSIONS FROM A FLIGHT FROM NY TO LA.

6,000

TIMES YOU CAN LISTEN TO THE HIT SONG "CAR WASH" ON A TWO HOUR FLIGHT.

30

1

DROPLETS EMITTED FROM A TOILET FLUSH.

7

MG OF MELATONIN TO RELAX.

35,000

MINUTES OF FREE IN-FLIGHT WIFI.

HOURS TIL YOUR PHONE DIES.

5

NUMBER OF FREE CARRY ONS.

1.73 METRIC TONS

MILES OF ALTITUDE BEFORE YOU CAN UNBUCKLE YOUR SEATBELT OR RUSH TO BATHROOM.

24

NUMBER OF DOLLARS A WATER COSTS IN THE TERMINAL.

15

SOLUTIONS

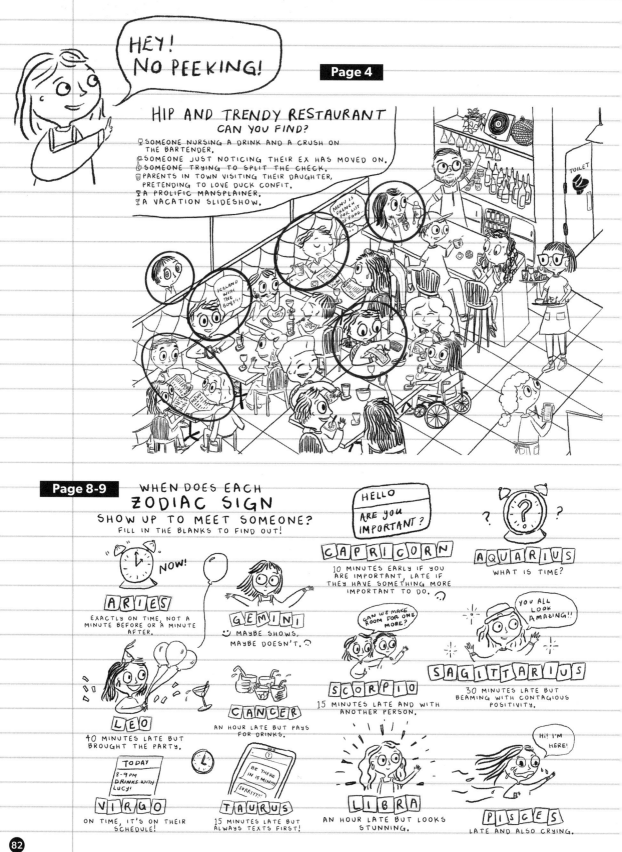

HEY! NO PEEKING!

Page 4

HIP AND TRENDY RESTAURANT
CAN YOU FIND?

- SOMEONE NURSING A DRINK AND A CRUSH ON THE BARTENDER.
- SOMEONE JUST NOTICING THEIR EX HAS MOVED ON.
- SOMEONE TRYING TO SPLIT THE CHECK.
- PARENTS IN TOWN VISITING THEIR DAUGHTER, PRETENDING TO LOVE DUCK CONFIT.
- A PROLIFIC MANSPLAINER.
- A VACATION SLIDESHOW.

Page 8-9

WHEN DOES EACH ZODIAC SIGN
SHOW UP TO MEET SOMEONE?
FILL IN THE BLANKS TO FIND OUT!

HELLO ARE YOU IMPORTANT?

CAPRICORN
10 MINUTES EARLY IF YOU ARE IMPORTANT, LATE IF THEY HAVE SOMETHING MORE IMPORTANT TO DO.

AQUARIUS
WHAT IS TIME?

ARIES
EXACTLY ON TIME, NOT A MINUTE BEFORE OR A MINUTE AFTER.

NOW!

GEMINI
MAYBE SHOWS, MAYBE DOESN'T.

CAN WE MAKE ROOM FOR ONE MORE?

SCORPIO
15 MINUTES LATE AND WITH ANOTHER PERSON.

YOU ALL LOOK AMAZING!!

SAGITTARIUS
30 MINUTES LATE BUT BEAMING WITH CONTAGIOUS POSITIVITY.

LEO
40 MINUTES LATE BUT BROUGHT THE PARTY.

CANCER
AN HOUR LATE BUT PAYS FOR DRINKS.

TODAY 8-9PM DRINKS WITH LUCY!

VIRGO
ON TIME, IT'S ON THEIR SCHEDULE!

BE THERE IN 15 MIN!!! SORRYYY!!

TAURUS
15 MINUTES LATE BUT ALWAYS TEXTS FIRST!

LIBRA
AN HOUR LATE BUT LOOKS STUNNING.

HI! I'M HERE!

PISCES
LATE AND ALSO CRYING.

Page 10-11

SPLIT THIS CHECK!

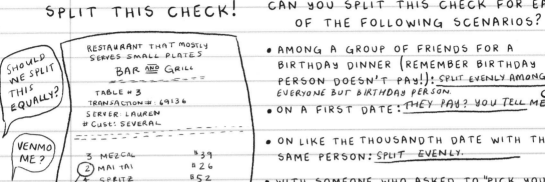

SHOULD WE SPLIT THIS EQUALLY?

VENMO ME?

YOUR ORDER!

WHAT'S THE TOTAL?

HOW MUCH FOR ME?

RESTAURANT THAT MOSTLY SERVES SMALL PLATES
BAR AND GRILL

TABLE # 3
TRANSACTION # 69136
SERVER: LAUREN
CUST: SEVERAL

3 MEZCAL	$39
2 MAI TAI	$26
4 SPRITZ	$52
1 NEGRONI	$16
1 CRISPY POTATOES	$9
2 HERB FRIES	$18
1 BRUSSELS	$11
1 CAULIFLOWER	$11
2 OYSTERS	$36
1 TARTINE BREAD	$14
3 SMOKED TROUT	$60
1 CHICKEN	$23
1 SHORT RIB	$29
1 CHOCOLATE TART	$11

TOTAL: $355
TIP: $71
INCLUDED
GRAND TOTAL: $426.00

CAN YOU SPLIT THIS CHECK FOR EACH OF THE FOLLOWING SCENARIOS?

- AMONG A GROUP OF FRIENDS FOR A BIRTHDAY DINNER (REMEMBER BIRTHDAY PERSON DOESN'T PAY!): SPLIT EVENLY AMONG EVERYONE BUT BIRTHDAY PERSON.

- ON A FIRST DATE: THEY PAY? YOU TELL ME.

- ON LIKE THE THOUSANDTH DATE WITH THE SAME PERSON: SPLIT EVENLY.

- WITH SOMEONE WHO ASKED TO "PICK YOUR BRAIN": LEAVE YOUR WALLET AT HOME. ☺

- WITH YOUR FRIEND WHO HAS BEEN SLEEPING ON YOUR COUCH FOR GOING ON TWO MONTHS: THEM?! MAYBE?

- AMONG A GROUP OF FRIENDS WHO ORDERED SOME THINGS FOR THE TABLE EVEN IF YOU DIDN'T EAT ANY OF IT.
   - IF YOU STILL WANT TO BE FRIENDS: SPLIT ☺
   - IF YOU DECIDE YOU DON'T REALLY LIKE THESE FRIENDS ANYMORE: ONLY PAY FOR WHAT YOU ATE ☹

Page 12-13

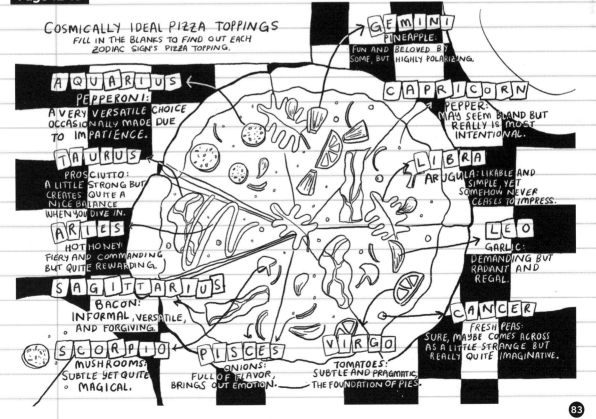

COSMICALLY IDEAL PIZZA TOPPINGS
FILL IN THE BLANKS TO FIND OUT EACH ZODIAC SIGN'S PIZZA TOPPING.

GEMINI
PINEAPPLE: FUN AND BELOVED BY SOME, BUT HIGHLY POLARIZING.

AQUARIUS
PEPPERONI: A VERY VERSATILE CHOICE OCCASIONALLY MADE DUE TO IMPATIENCE.

CAPRICORN
PEPPER: MAY SEEM BLAND BUT REALLY IS MOST INTENTIONAL.

TAURUS
PROSCIUTTO: A LITTLE STRONG BUT CREATES QUITE A NICE BALANCE WHEN YOU DIVE IN.

LIBRA
ARUGULA: LIKABLE AND SIMPLE, YET SOMEHOW NEVER CEASES TO IMPRESS.

ARIES
HOT HONEY: FIERY AND COMMANDING BUT QUITE REWARDING.

LEO
GARLIC: DEMANDING BUT RADIANT AND REGAL.

SAGITTARIUS
BACON: INFORMAL, VERSATILE, AND FORGIVING.

CANCER
FRESH PEAS: SURE, MAYBE COMES ACROSS AS A LITTLE STRANGE BUT REALLY QUITE IMAGINATIVE.

SCORPIO
MUSHROOMS: SUBTLE YET QUITE MAGICAL.

PISCES
ONIONS: FULL OF FLAVOR, BRINGS OUT EMOTION.

VIRGO
TOMATOES: SUBTLE AND PRAGMATIC, THE FOUNDATION OF PIES.

Page 40-41

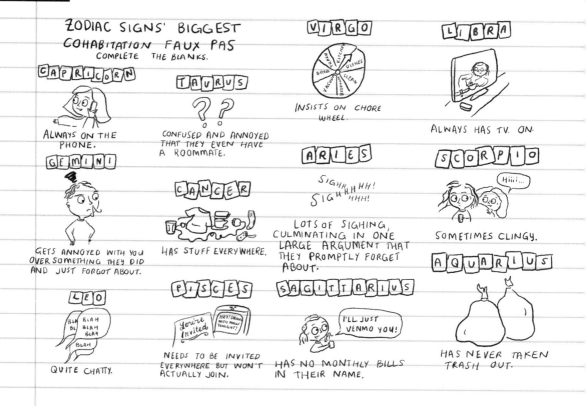

Page 44-45

Page 46-47

COFFEE BY ZODIAC SIGN
FILL IN THE BLANKS TO FIND OUT HOW EACH ZODIAC SIGN GETS THEIR CAFFEINE.

CAPRICORN

ESPRESSO: CLASSIC AND EFFICIENT.

AQUARIUS

OAT MILK — BUT FIRST... COFFEE!

COFFEE WITH OAT MILK: TRENDY

PISCES

INSTANT COFFEE: IMPATIENT BUT NOT PICKY.

SAGITTARIUS

DECAF: DOESN'T NEED CAFFEINE.

LIBRA

POUR OVER: VERY PATIENT.

SCORPIO

RED EYE: VERY INTENSE.

VIRGO

SPECIAL MUG

DRIP COFFEE WITH 2 SUGARS: ROUTINE CHOICE.

LEO

NESPRESSO: FLASHY AND VERY IMPATIENT.

GEMINI

COLD BREW: FUN! SUMMER FOREVER!

CANCER

LATTE: SOFT AND SWEET.

TAURUS

KEURIG: DEPENDABLE.

ARIES

FRENCH PRESS: VERY STRONG.

Page 50

EXCUSE ME — CAN YOU WATCH MY THINGS?
DRAW AN ARROW TO SEE WHO'S WATCHING WHOSE THINGS TO FIGURE OUT WHOSE STUFF IS UNATTENDED.

WELL MAYBE NOW YOU CAN WATCH MY THINGS?

JUST FOR A SEC...?

UNATTENDED!

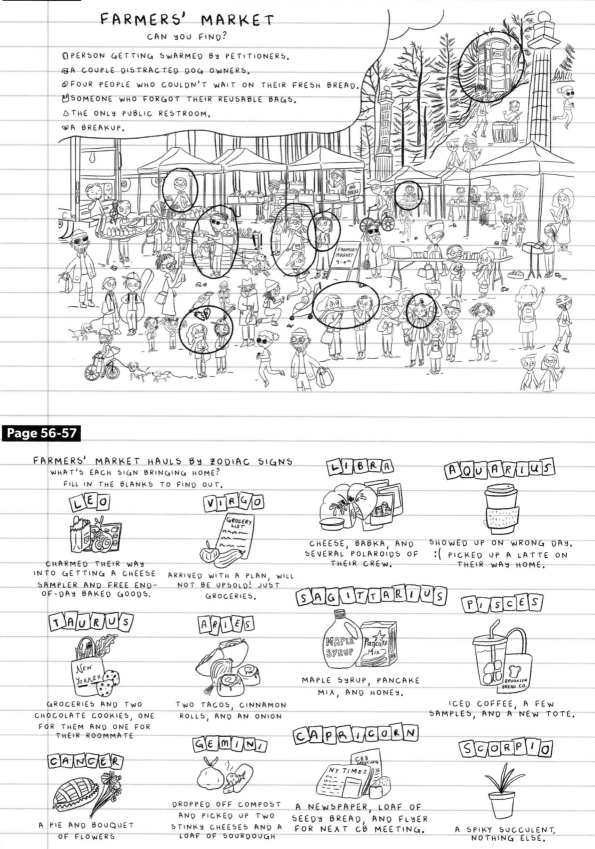

SOLUTIONS

Page 54-55

FARMERS' MARKET

CAN YOU FIND?

1 PERSON GETTING SWARMED BY PETITIONERS.
2 A COUPLE DISTRACTED DOG OWNERS.
3 FOUR PEOPLE WHO COULDN'T WAIT ON THEIR FRESH BREAD.
4 SOMEONE WHO FORGOT THEIR REUSABLE BAGS.
5 THE ONLY PUBLIC RESTROOM.
6 A BREAKUP.

Page 56-57

FARMERS' MARKET HAULS BY ZODIAC SIGNS

WHAT'S EACH SIGN BRINGING HOME?
FILL IN THE BLANKS TO FIND OUT.

LEO — CHARMED THEIR WAY INTO GETTING A CHEESE SAMPLER AND FREE END-OF-DAY BAKED GOODS.

VIRGO — ARRIVED WITH A PLAN, WILL NOT BE UPSOLD! JUST GROCERIES.

LIBRA — CHEESE, BABKA, AND SEVERAL POLAROIDS OF THEIR CREW.

AQUARIUS — SHOWED UP ON WRONG DAY. :(PICKED UP A LATTE ON THEIR WAY HOME.

TAURUS — GROCERIES AND TWO CHOCOLATE COOKIES, ONE FOR THEM AND ONE FOR THEIR ROOMMATE

ARIES — TWO TACOS, CINNAMON ROLLS, AND AN ONION

SAGITTARIUS — MAPLE SYRUP, PANCAKE MIX, AND HONEY.

PISCES — ICED COFFEE, A FEW SAMPLES, AND A NEW TOTE.

CANCER — A PIE AND BOUQUET OF FLOWERS

GEMINI — DROPPED OFF COMPOST AND PICKED UP TWO STINKY CHEESES AND A LOAF OF SOURDOUGH

CAPRICORN — A NEWSPAPER, LOAF OF SEEDY BREAD, AND FLYER FOR NEXT CB MEETING.

SCORPIO — A SPIKY SUCCULENT, NOTHING ELSE.

Page 69

CIRCLE THE ITEMS A DOG
SHOULD NOT EAT UNDER ANY
CIRCUMSTANCES!

(FROM A HUMAN'S, NOT A DOG'S, PERSPECTIVE, OBVIOUSLY!)

CHOCOLATE BAR — CHOCOLATE

STREET FOOD

GUM

AVOCADO

RAISINS

CARROTS

BANANA

YOUR DINNER

SHOELACES

BEEF

POOP

SHOES

HEY — HAVE YOU SEEN MY DINNER?

Page 70-71

AIRPORT TERMINAL

CAN YOU FIND?

• A MISPLACED PASSPORT.

• AN OPEN OUTLET NEAR A CHAIR OR SOME FLOOR SPACE TO CHARGE YOUR PHONE.

• UNATTENDED LUGGAGE. TSK, TSK!

• SOMEONE HEADING TO PARADISE.

• A FORGOTTEN BELT.

• A COMFORT ANIMAL? OR A PARROT?

DETROIT 10:05ᴬᴹ

NEW ORLEANS NOW DEPARTING 9:00

EXIT

GATE 73

GATE 75

← BAGGAGE
GATES 4-20

Page 72-73

ZODIAC SIGNS' BOARDING TENDENCIES
FILL IN THE BLANKS TO FIND OUT THE
BOARDING TENDENCIES OF EACH ZODIAC SIGN.

CANCER
PRE-CHECK
BOARDING PASS
HAS PRE-CHECK!

PISCES
GATE 81
FLIGHT TO LAX
NOW BOARDING
STANDS BY GATE AS SOON AS
ANNOUNCEMENT IS MADE.

ARIES
STAYS SEATED UNTIL GROUP
IS CALLED, BUT THEN POWERS
RIGHT TO THE FRONT OF THE
LINE.

GEMINI
GATE 7
BOARDS AS GATE CLOSES.

LEO
FIRST CLASS, WAITING IN THE
LOUNGE.

AQUARIUS
GATE 78
OH NO.
WAITS PATIENTLY TO BOARD
THEN REALIZES THEY ARE
WAITING AT WRONG GATE.

TAURUS
WAITS NEAR BOARDING AREA
TEN MINUTES BEFORE IT
STARTS.

SAGITTARIUS
FIRST IS
THE WORST...
SOMEHOW ALWAYS LAST BUT
NOT STRESSED ABOUT IT.

VIRGO
ARRIVES WITH PLENTY OF TIME TO
USE THE RESTROOM, FILL THEIR
WATER, AND WAIT PATIENTLY
WITHOUT CROWDING ANYONE.

CAPRICORN
BUSINESS,
BUSINESS,
YES...
SECOND ONLY TO FIRST
CLASS, WHILE ON A CALL.

SCORPIO
GROUP 4
ON MY
BOARDING
PASS, GROUP
1 IN MY
HEAD.
WILL BOARD WHENEVER THEY
CHOOSE.

LIBRA
ARE WE NOW
BEST FRIENDS?
STARTED A CONVERSATION
WITH ANOTHER TRAVELER AND
NOW IS MAYBE UPGRADED?

Page 75

WHAT'S SETTING OFF
SECURITY?

CAN YOU LOCATE ALL THE ITEMS THAT ARE SETTING OFF
SECURITY?

X-RAYS?

I ONLY HAD
SPACE FOR MY
EMOTIONAL
BAGGAGE.

SHOULD WE
"UNPACK" IT?

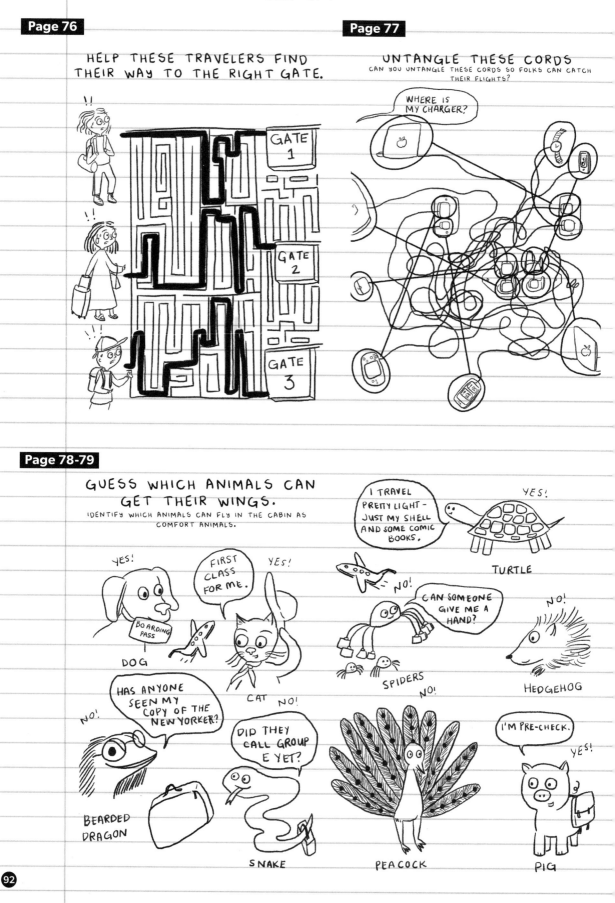

Page 81

CAN YOU PAIR EACH OF THESE WITH THE CORRECT NUMBER?

NO NEED TO BE A MATHEMATICIAN HERE, TRUST YOUR GUT!

CARBON EMISSIONS FROM A FLIGHT FROM NY TO LA.

TIMES YOU CAN LISTEN TO THE HIT SONG "CAR WASH" ON A TWO HOUR FLIGHT.

DROPLETS EMITTED FROM A TOILET FLUSH.

MG OF MELATONIN TO RELAX.

MINUTES OF FREE IN-FLIGHT WIFI.

HOURS TIL YOUR PHONE DIES.

NUMBER OF FREE CARRY ONS.

MILES OF ALTITUDE BEFORE YOU CAN UNBUCKLE YOUR SEATBELT OR RUSH TO BATHROOM.

NUMBER OF DOLLARS A WATER COSTS IN THE TERMINAL.

6,000

30

1

7

35,000

5

1.73 METRIC TONS

24

15

NEED SOLUTIONS FOR ANYTHING ELSE?

FOLLOW YOUR HEART.

YOU DO YOU.

ABOUT THE AUTHOR
CAN YOU FIND:

- AUTHOR HEADSHOT
- FURRY COLLABORATOR
- PHONE CHARGER

SARAH KEMPA IS A CARTOONIST WITH WORK APPEARING IN THE NEW YORKER, MCSWEENEY'S, AND MORE. YOU CAN FIND MORE CARTOONS ON INSTAGRAM @auntsarahdraws OR SHOP HER STORE ON ETSY www.etsy.com/shop/auntsarahdraws.